IN DEFENSE OF OBEDIENCE

AND

REFLECTIONS ON THE PRIESTHOOD

By Anne, a lay apostle

In Defense of Obedience and Reflections on the Priesthood

By Anne, a lay apostle

ISBN: 1-933684-45-3
Library of Congress Number Applied For

Publisher:
Direction for Our Times

Manufactured in the United States of America

Copy of painting of *Jesus Christ the Returning King* by Janusz Antosz, reproduced with permission.

Direction for Our Times
9000 West 81st Street
Justice, Illinois 60458

www.directionforourtimes.com

Email: contactus@directionforourtimes.com
Phone: 708-496-9300

Direction For Our Times — Ireland
Lisnalea
Virginia Rd.
Bailieborough
Co. Cavan.
Republic of Ireland

www.directionforourtimes.com

Email: dfotireland@yahoo.ie
Phone: 353-(0)42-969-4947

Jesus gives Anne a message for the world on
the first of each month. To receive the
monthly messages you may access our website at
www.directionforourtimes.com
or call us at one of the phone numbers listed
above to be placed on our mailing list.

Direction for Our Times wishes to manifest its complete obedience and submission of mind and heart to the final and definitive judgment of the Magisterium of the Catholic Church and the local Ordinary regarding the supernatural character of the messages received by Anne, a lay apostle.

In this spirit, the messages of Anne, a lay apostle, have been submitted to her bishop, Most Reverend Leo O'Reilly, Bishop of Kilmore, Ireland, and to the Vatican Congregation for the Doctrine of the Faith for formal examination. In the meantime Bishop O'Reilly has given permission for their publication.

Table of Contents

In Defense of Obedience

Spring 2007
Jesus

My beloved apostles seek to serve Me in each moment. This gives Me cause to rejoice. My heart lifts especially at any act of obedience made to the authority I have placed with the Church. I intend to unify all apostles serving in this time. If your heart is with Me, your Jesus, you will feel the urge to align yourself in humility to the decisions made by the authority of the Church. It is this that I ask of you. It is this that I require from you. My beloved ones, it is this that will increase the speed of the renewal. Rest often in My Eucharistic heart. There you will find the discernment you need to abandon any path of disobedience that is leading you away from My will. Perhaps this is not a concern for you because you are already respectful of My authority in the Church. This is good. But if change is necessary for you, you may be assured that I will not leave you without prompting and guidance. You seek liberation from any self-will that draws you from Me. I, also, seek this for you. Perhaps you feel that your life cannot be changed immediately but you are willing to embark on a process of change to adjust your course. Be at peace. It is I who prompts the course adjustment. I will see to it if you allow Me.

In Defense of Obedience

In this period of history, as in every period, there exist many realities which call for change. Human beings must always seek to perfect their behavior toward each other and this continuing process of improving man's condition is positive and necessary and, I believe, blessed and ordained by God. This stated, I believe that certain current attempts to improve mankind have spiralled into a widespread spirit of disobedience.

The concept of obedience is not a popular one during this time. More popular concepts include choice, freedom, and liberation. But do we really accept that people have the choice to hurt others and the freedom to sin without correction? And from whom do we wish to be liberated? From God?

How could good intentions have gone so badly wrong leaving us in this present sad condition? In response to those who object to the description of our condition on earth as sad, let me say that I am speaking from the standpoint of one who seeks to see with the eyes of Our Lord, Jesus Christ, who loves mankind and ordains peace and self-acceptance in all followers. I do not see peace in most people. I do not see in people an awareness of their bountiful dignity. It is my belief that a great many of God's children lack self-acceptance.

This is not a fruit of unity with God but of disunity, which I believe comes in part from a spirit of disobedience.

Why obey? How much should one obey? Should one obey sometimes? All the time? When one agrees with the given instruction? Should one obey when one disagrees? Should one go against one's better judgment in order to obey?

It is not the goal of this writing to make judgments on any individual. I will have to examine this concept in terms of my own experience and trust the Lord to shed light on it if He so wills.

There have been many times in my life when I was tempted to disobedience. First, there was a period of time when I lived away from the sacraments. I made rebellious decisions and kept non-Christian company. I suffered commensurately and it soon became clear to me that the world did not love me. I was mercifully drawn back to Jesus, through Mary, and He provided for me spiritually, mentally and emotionally.

Later, when I had returned to the Church, I struggled on another level. It was a process to align my life personally to the Lord's will and the teachings of the Church. I knew that I had to do so, however, and I embarked on the process.

During this time of personal struggle, I also experienced a temptation to systemic disobedience against the Church.

The Church gives clear teaching on birth control and contraception but science has advanced in such a way that we can generally prevent conception when we wish to do so. I worked in the women's movement and saw horrific exploitation and abuse of women and their children. It was difficult for me to reconcile myself to the Church's teaching at first. I understood that I was called to obey personally, but I was not convinced that this teaching was best for everyone. I lacked knowledge. Once I obtained the knowledge and understood the Lord's plan for women, I began to see that it was disobedience, not Church teaching, that threatened the well-being of women and children. The Church's teaching provides protection for the dignity of women and children and the Natural Family Planning Method is scientific and safe for women. God's way is the right way and I believe the Church is acting according to God's will in these matters.

If one openly disobeys a Church teaching, one is in essence saying that one wants the responsibility of leadership, which God has not given. One is, through disobedience, wresting authority. I believe that God puts Church leaders in positions of responsibility with the hope that they will obey the Church authority, helping them to grow in personal holiness and furthering unity in the Church.

We must accept that we may not understand everything about each directive we are called to follow. We may not have all of the facts. God treats some things on a 'need to know' basis.

One could observe that individuals will only disobey when they feel the Church authority in their life is getting it wrong. Most of the time, perhaps, they will obey. But where does this end? And if this is the case, then nobody is in charge, least of all God. I fear that those who cut and paste in the area of obedience to the Magisterium will find themselves in a position where their peace is destroyed and their effectiveness, from heaven's perspective, is diminished.

God can't count on them. They might obey, they might not. This disposition threatens His plan.

Decisions against the Church give satan ammunition to use against us in our movement to personal holiness, which is our base mission here on earth regardless of who we are. The enemy uses this ammunition, our uncertainty and consequent vulnerability, to teach us about arrogance and to distract us from holiness. If we make a decision against the authority of the Church, we will have to spend a lot of time justifying it. We will possibly lie awake in bed at night arguing with nobody in order to prove to ourselves that we are right. We may come to know outrage, which fuels arrogance. Yes, we will exhaust ourselves trying to convince ourselves that we are right or, at the very least, justified in our disobedience.

Be alert. Satan will send people to support and encourage us in disobedience. We can always find someone who agrees with us. We must not seek the companionship of those who pull from unity with the Church. We must seek instead the counsel of those who encourage unity. These souls will have suffered. Their obedience will usually have cost them something and from these we will receive calm and wise counsel.

I understand that life is not black and white. I understand that many Church leaders cite compassion as a reason to disobey. They state, and possibly believe, that they are acting positively in response to the pain of their people. I understand this because I experienced the same thing in the women's movement. Despite this, I believe that the most compassionate assistance we can provide to others is the knowledge of God's truth and mercy in His teachings and the knowledge of God's continued presence in this world. Can we in good conscience deny truth to others in the name of mercy? Do we feel that God has denied others the capability and capacity for holiness?

Possibly at this time we disagree with a Church teaching or with the manner in which a Church teaching is being implemented. We are all thinking individuals after all and have the right to think in any way we like. We cannot stop our minds from consideration and it is often through consideration that we become reconciled and convicted.

Also, it is clear that each region and congregation experiences unique challenges and each individual will find his own struggle in his own mission field.

But I would say that Church leaders have a profound call to

illustrate a spirit of obedience to the Magisterium for followers using the Church's teaching in the Catechism for guidance.

All must accept that there are times when we are not in charge, when we are called to follow, not lead, or if you will, to lead by following the authority.

Only if we remain small can God's bigness be seen. If we try to be big, we will obstruct the view others have of God.

At times, if we are to be obedient, we will have to make decisions against our personal will. We should expect this. As I said, we may even be called to make a decision to obey even though we may feel that the person in authority is mistaken. This is difficult indeed, perhaps the most difficult thing, but the fact that we are willing to do so illustrates humility, a trembling, a faith in a divine intellect that is greater than our own and a plan that is bigger than our own.

These decisions, the heroic acts of obedience, will put God in the absolute position of answering with His limitless power and I believe that the Lord is incapable of disappointing obedience.

As always, let us look to His example. Our beloved one was "obedient even unto death" (Phil. 2:8). How palatable could the plan that was the Passion have seemed to the eternal victim? How sensible could it have appeared to His mother? Or His followers? Should Peter have persisted and cut down the soldiers who came to arrest Jesus? Should he have disobeyed, using his better judgment? Jesus said no and Peter stood down. The plan, the divine plan, unfolded in all its apparent senselessness.

God's plan was unfathomable to His apostles. This act of total sacrifice denied human rationale. Yes, on that day, it is abundantly clear that God's plan mystified His followers.

We must accept that like the early apostles, on any given day God's plan will mystify us. We are, after all, no better than our predecessors.

Our call to obedience is often a call to the heroic in terms of humility and faith.

To be clear, I am not advocating mindless servility. I am advocating fidelity to the decision we have all made to serve Jesus Christ, according to His plan, in His Church.

Obedience is liberating in many ways.

First of all, it frees our mind. We do not have to wonder what to do in most given situations. If we cooperate with the authority in our life, Jesus can move us to holiness with great speed. If we do not cooperate, we do not allow Jesus to direct, and He will have to go slowly with us, in order to protect us. His goals will be jeopardized.

It is distressing to witness a spirit of pride and arrogance. We must always look for personal outrage as a marker for pride in ourselves. By this I do not refer to the outrage one feels regarding injustice done to others. This is appropriate. By this, the marker for pride, I refer to personal outrage associated with being treated less respectfully than we would like or being judged in a way that is less positive than we feel we deserve or desire. To clarify, we can go, as usual, to the Lord's example.

When people lied about Jesus personally or mistreated Him, He let it go, as in the Garden. He did not puff up and sputter in outrage. He was very consistent in behaving like a lamb.

But when people planned to stone an adulteress, He stopped them. He exhibited a sense of outrage, turning the situation on its head and using it to promote non-judgmental treatment of others.

Also, when He witnessed His Father's house being used as a market place, He exhibited outrage, even reacting with just anger.

Jesus quietly accepted personal insults and slights to Himself. He did not accept cruel behavior against people or blasphemous behavior against His Father.

There are those who will say that to behave in obedience is to offer up our free will. This is true. This is what we are striving for, to offer up our free will to the Lord. It is only when we give up trying to be masters that we can become servants. We will not enter heaven with our hands on our hips, telling everyone else, least of all Christ, where they are getting it wrong.

The former Holy Father, Pope John Paul II, made a statement on the ordination of women. In summary he said, "No. It's not going to happen." He issued an Apostolic Letter called *Ordinatio Sacerdotalis* detailing his thoughts. One of the observations he made was that surely if Jesus wanted women to be priests, He would have made His mother a priest. He did not. Jesus protected the separate and distinct roles of men and women in the Church. Nearly two thousand years later, the Holy Father Pope John Paul II protected the Lord's will by steering the Church in the direction God desired.

Some objected to the definitive nature of the Apostolic Letter. Then Cardinal Ratzinger made a statement that the matter should no longer be discussed. Waves of outrage erupted. How dare this man tell us what we can and cannot discuss?

This baffles me. Cardinal Ratzinger's statement seems to be an appropriate statement for a man of obedience attempting to support the correct and proper authority in his Church. I do not understand what others did not understand about this.

The fact that people wanted to continue discussing the matter after a definitive statement by the only appropriate authority is, in itself, evidence of a spirit of disobedience.

This is much like my children arguing over which movie we are going to see after I have stated definitively that we are not going to the cinema. The discussion is a waste of time and evidence that either their hearing is impaired or they are fighting for the sake of fighting.

Rather than be outraged, would it not have been better to think, in humility, Hmm. The Holy Father is serious about this. No doubt he has his reasons.

Would it not be wise to accept that God did not abandon the Holy Father with this important decision regarding the direction of His Church on earth?

Those of us who nourish similar outrage are wasting valuable time during which we are supposed to be working on our own movement to unity with Jesus and saving souls.

There are two paths. There is God's way, the path to personal holiness which is marked out by obedience and a spirit of humility. And there is the other way, satan's path, which is marked out by pride and possibly grudging, bitter obedience, which leads to outright disobedience. Be aware that the spirit of personal outrage in us is always being stoked by the enemy in order to distract us from the job at hand, which is the divine will in each moment.

When we feel personal outrage we must run to Jesus immediately. This will prevent us from doing anything ridiculous or damaging.

With obedience comes humility and with humility comes obedience. You might say one feeds the other. Again, this does not mean we cannot question decisions or requests. It is normal to seek clarity when we do not understand. But we must do so respectfully, mindful of the presence of God in others and careful not to influence others to doubt. Those who challenge in arrogance know what I am saying and those whose spirit is false and duplicitous are known to God. How often the enemy speaks with pretend innocence and with no intention of accepting God's clarity. How often the enemy sets up a holy man for ambush. The enemy thinks he is very clever indeed but God reads souls, my friends. He knows what is in our hearts.

Now, if we are quite certain that a given human authority claiming to represent the Church has it wrong, clearly we have a dilemma and because we are dealing with humanity this can happen. In such times we must be very prayerful, saying, "Jesus, surely You are aware that You have a problem here."

We must speak our conscience honestly, respectfully and privately to the authority in question and then leave the Lord to get on with His job, continuing on our walk to personal holiness via the path of obedience. Spiritual direction in these situations is invaluable.

To be sure, there will be times when we wonder if the Lord knows what He is doing. Doubts and fears will come. We may feel certain that the Lord's plan unfolding before us cannot possibly be successful. This is consistent with our humanity and consequent lack of divine vision. Our service in the face of these fears gives delight to God. But we must go along with God. If indeed our obedience and the decisions made by certain Church authorities result in disaster, it is the Lord's problem.

If we obey, if we decide for obedience and then walk hard and steady up that path, we will be free to become saints.

To retain a spirit of obedience, one must nourish an intimate relationship with Jesus Christ. It should be very personal to us, this relationship, because it is very personal to Him. All of our days should be spent in the awareness that we are in the presence of the Lord, who lays great stock in our acceptance of His will.

Jesus has plans and goals. He has designed in advance what He can do with our "yes" answer. His plan deals always with the salvation of our own soul, of course, but then Jesus works tirelessly for our loved ones and if we say "yes" to Him, He takes that "yes" and sees to our personal intentions first. This benevolence alone should melt us into willing servants.

There is Jesus Christ. We work to gain and retain unity with Him. This occurs through our willingness to do things His way.

Then there is the Father, who radiates the divine will, perfect goodness. Between Jesus and the Father there is a stream, this divine will, an active, living, fluid exchange. The Holy Spirit is moving constantly between the two, connecting them. If we are united to Jesus through our willingness, He places us in this stream of light that connects us to the Godhead. As far as we are willing to advance in holiness through our "yes" answers to God, Jesus advances us.

I believe that it is obedience that anchors us in this stream.

In this time, I see arrogance and superiority. I do not know about other times so I cannot speak of whether or not arrogance has increased or decreased or whether or not it is more prevalent or less prevalent than yesterday, but I can say that I see a lot of it now. The Lord has told me that this age is more disobedient than other ages and I believe Him.

To return to arrogance, there is a spirit of intellectual superiority that emits a steady flow of sarcasm. This is distasteful to Jesus. Better we limit our study to flowers in fields than contribute to this embarrassing and serious phenomenon that puts so many people off and limits the Holy Spirit. Many have educated themselves right out of reach of the Spirit. They say, in summary, "No thank you. I have no need for silent contemplation. You see, I have higher learning."

I am not objecting to higher learning and study. How could I when it opens the door to so many delightful possibilities? I am objecting to arrogance, superiority and spiritual suffocation. It is not Jesus Christ or the Holy Spirit encouraging people to believe they are superior to others. It is God's enemy.

Those who read with humility will question themselves in this area. The Lord wants us to understand that even those with the highest learning on earth will find themselves pitifully unprepared for heaven if they do not contemplate daily how little they know. I have heard it said that only a truly wise man understands the depth of his ignorance. I believe this to be true.

To see a man with a lively intellect, with great learning, and with humility is surely a delight to the heart of our Savior.

Education, and everything else in our lives, should bring us closer to God and closer to obedience. If we find that we are moving away from obedience, noted by a feeling of superiority to those who obey, we must be alerted. We should embark on a course of Eucharistic Adoration, simply contemplating Jesus Christ in the Sacrament of the Altar. We must learn to love and we must learn from the Master.

If we do this, we will gradually begin to listen more and talk less. We will be less sure of our own opinions, open to the idea that we could be wrong about some things even while we are right about others. We will be more likely to accept the authority of those God has placed in our lives to lead us. We will come to allow others to fight the fight of words while we fight the fight of the spirit, the fight of holiness.

Dear friends, we must scrutinize ourselves. This is not an area where we want to get it wrong. If we generally believe we know more than others, we must turn toward the Lord and allow Him to educate or possibly re-educate our spirit.

A case in point is a wife and mother who recently told me that she was not very religious. She said that she had not read a great deal of religious books and therefore had little knowledge of things religious. I had, over time, opportunity to observe this woman with her children, her husband and in her life.

I said to her, "You may not be very religious, but you are extremely holy."

This baffled her.

I have met Church scholars who were very religious. They quoted learning from the early centuries and back, right up to the present. They knew lots of things that this wife and mother did not. I believe though, that if she were taken up to heaven right now, she would more or less fit in because she is all about service and love. She is all about sacrifice and humility. She is all about gentleness and respect for children and for the emotional protection of her husband, honoring the trust that he has placed in her through their marriage.

It has to be stated. This woman, according to heaven's goals which place personal sanctity first, is doing better.

Holiness is not a competition, of course. We only compete against our performance in the last five minutes, meaning we each need to try to do better than we have in the past. But look at what God must overcome in the wife and mother and then compare it to what God must overcome in the scholar.

Knowledge is not necessary for holiness. Humility is.

The wife does not think she is superior. She feels she must do better because she is not very religious. For the record, this woman never misses Sunday Mass and provides beautifully for the formation of her children. She lives in obedience to the Church. By religious she means saying the Rosary daily, reading religious works, and saying novenas and going on pilgrimages.

The scholar, on the other hand, is disdainful of this woman.

He feels miles above her. He would not deign to speak to her for any length of time because he feels certain she is beneath him. If he would listen and observe, he would understand what this woman could teach him because she, through practice, has learned about prudence and generosity, kindness and forgiveness. She is actively practicing virtue and growing in holiness. She truly grasps religious concepts in her heart even though she lacks the words to describe them.

This, my friends, is the difference between running and talking about running. She is exerting herself. The scholar in this discussion is not.

I believe God is pleased with this woman and I believe God is hopeful that this scholar will learn humility.

Priests, in particular, must be wary of a spirit of superiority. Humility is very important to God's goals for their vocation.

To quote from the previously mentioned apostolic letter *Ordinatio Sacerdotalis* of Pope John Paul II to the Bishops of the Catholic Church on Reserving Priestly Ordination to Men Alone, *"Moreover, it is to the holiness and the faithful that the hierarchical structure of the Church is totally ordered. For this reason, the Declaration Inter Insigniores recalls: "the only better gift, which can and must be desired, is love (cf.1 Cor 12 and 13). The greatest in the Kingdom of Heaven are not the ministers but the saints (par. 3).*

A first observation is that God wills that through their vocations, all priests become saints, but it must be underscored that the whole point of the priest's learning is to help God to raise up saints. This woman is part of the Body of Christ. She, and all individuals like her, are the point. One could say that her advancement in holiness is the goal for the priest's vocation and all that God puts into the priest's vocation should direct him that way. He is to minister to and thereby raise up saints, all the while admiring and standing in reverence of the grace present in those to whom he ministers. I pray for God's clarity in this point as it is so important for the humility of all priests.

With a trembling spirit I will say it this way. If a priest, of any level of authority in the Church, holds himself above those to whom he is called to minister, he needs to adjust his thinking.

We must not make a false god of education and learning or allow education and learning to persuade us that we ourselves are gods. We must use education and learning to examine our condition in relation to the example of Jesus Christ.

The authority with which a person speaks is the love and presence of Christ in his words. Knowledge is good, if it includes the presence and love of Jesus Christ.

Back to obedience, we can speak about obedience to God's Church and be technically correct but lack God's authority if we speak without God's love.

So perhaps there are two parts to obedience. There is obedience to the letter of the law and obedience to the spirit of the law. When one is missing, the other falters.

To take it further, if a Church leader acts in opposition to the authority of the Church, even given a stated intention of compassion and even assuming true compassion, he acts with only partial authority because he is acting without the letter of the law. If he acts in obedience to the Church and to the letter of the law but without the spirit of the law, which is God's love, he also lacks God's authority because he is acting in a manner inconsistent with the example of Jesus Christ.

One, love without obedience, or the other, obedience without love, produces incongruity that confuses the faithful and damages their trust in their priests, their Church, and by extension, their God.

Also, the Catholic Church must demonstrate unity and consistency for our brothers and sisters of other faiths who watch us closely and to whom we owe, by heavenly obligation, a good example.

Clearly, the faithful in the Church rely on Church leaders for direction. The Church does not point to itself, but rather to Jesus Christ and to each individual's movement to unity with Jesus Christ. Since eternity in heaven for the faithful consists of and rests upon unity with Jesus Christ, then unity with Jesus Christ must be the compelling goal for the faithful. The Church, by heavenly design, encourages and promotes this unity.

When a Church leader takes a public position against the Magisterium, or even preaches in such a way that sows doubt about the Magisterium, the message promoted is that the Catholic Church, and by extension Jesus Christ, is getting it wrong. This seriously erodes confidence in the Church, and by extension, Jesus Christ.

This doubt creates fear and anxiety in all the faithful, lay and clergy alike, because it strikes deeply into the heart of our trust in the Lord. Spiritually, many souls are distracted and stumble. This creates an opening for the enemy to violently shake the tree of our confidence in Christ and many fruits that the Lord has taken years to cultivate can fall from our souls to the ground, to rot and decay.

Disunity becomes apparent because some fall prey to confusion. Others, perhaps better rooted in obedience, will hold the line. There will be conflict though, a positioning of one against another. We begin to resemble the enemy's legion, bickering and undermining each other, tearing off in this direction or that one.

Also, the public disobedience of some leaves the clergy and faithful who hold the line vulnerable. They may be marked as cold, uncaring, out of touch, and lacking compassion. Their authentic message of the Good News is weakened because some, confused by the disobedience of others, distrust their motives and fail to correctly identify the truth.

Those who depart from obedience, even allowing for the motive of compassion, are stating, albeit maybe indirectly, that the Church, and again and always by extension, Jesus Christ, are not compassionate but they, the disobedient ones, are. They are standing with their back to Christ, drawing attention to themselves as the Savior, the Merciful One. They are drawing souls to themselves instead of directing souls to Jesus Christ. In doing so, they block the faithful's rightful view of God, who is the true source of all goodness and mercy.

To make an obvious observation, the humanity of each person insures that the presence of each person is temporary. Eventually all people depart, through relocation, retirement or death. If disobedient people have placed themselves as the draw, the goal for the faithful, their departure leaves a gaping hole where Jesus Christ, represented by the Church, should have been placed. I have seen this happen.

Clergy taking a public position of disobedience to the Church are encouraging the faithful to build their homes on unsteady ground. They are attaching their flock's spiritual security to themselves. Which man is steady enough, wise enough, and powerful enough to do such a thing? Only one Man existed who possessed these traits to perfection. He, Jesus Christ, has gone before us.

God wills that Catholics proceed always deeper into personal holiness through the path marked for them personally within the safe pasture of the Catholic Church. If the example set for Catholics by representatives of the Church is faulty and flawed, the faithful will be misdirected and misguided.

In this time, God wills that we move from an Age of Disobedience to an Age of Obedience. Think of this like a big boulder that must be shifted to another designated place. If we are to successfully shift this boulder and move it to the place God wills, we will need to act in unison. If part of the Body of Christ remains on the opposite side pushing against the faithful, the boulder will not move and we are exhausting ourselves, from the standpoint of the renewal, to no purpose.

Consequently, it is in our best interest, and clearly within God's will, that we assist our brothers and sisters in coming to the place of obedience, in both the letter and spirit of God's directions, made known to us through the authority of His Church.

Be warned. We must be compassionate in this effort and humble and merciful, but when dialoguing with those who are in error through disobedience, we must be certain that we stick to the intended goal which is to bring them to obedience, in both spirit and letter, and not the opposite, which would be allowing them to bring us to disobedience.

Silent contemplation of the Eucharist is, I believe, necessary for us so that we can hold God's line steady for Him and not be tempted to join the ones pushing against the boulder, that is, God's renewal.

As a caution, there exist subtle snares laid by the enemy. When one is confronted by genuine compassion in those acting against the Magisterium, one can be drawn into confusion. Many of these souls make excellent points in that there are areas in the Church which I believe the Lord wants improved. I see that the Lord is conducting change in these matters but through respectful dialogue, not rebellion. If I were curious to know what the Lord was concerned about in the Church, I would look at the Holy Father and see what areas are of concern to him.

Clearly, we must consider the return to obedience a process. Perhaps what is called for is a movement to obedience, a gentle shifting, directed by heaven, from one place to another.

God has willed a great renewal. It will happen. It is happening now.

We each have a role, willed by God, to play in this renewal.

This renewal will not advance through pride and disobedience. This renewal will advance through unity, which will be achieved through humility and obedience.

If you are rebelling against God's Church, I beg you, stand down.

"First of all, obedience is apostolic, in the sense that it recognizes, loves and serves the Church in her hierarchical structure" (P.73 *Pastores Dabo Vobis*, *Apostolic exhortation of His Holiness John Paul II on the formation of Priests).*

Reflections On the Priesthood

Reflections On the Priesthood

A priest makes a decision to enter into the relationship of knowing God, of seeking Him. Through this decision, Jesus is able to possess the priest as an outpost, a dwelling place for the Godhead on earth.

With God's grace, I can see Christ in the priest on his ordination day and I can see Christ in the priest on the day of his death. I have also seen Christ in priests in heaven. They all look the same to me in that Christ is Christ on the ordination day, the day of death, and into and for eternity. So while the priest moves through his life in humanity, with doubts and imperfections, Jesus has no doubts and imperfections. Jesus serves humanity through the priest in His perfect divinity. I am as delighted by Christ in the priesthood as I am by Christ in the words He sends or Christ in the Eucharist or Christ in the heavenly experiences of Him that I have been allowed to have. It is for this reason, I believe, I feel such love for priests, regardless of their condition.

Given this, the Lord's mystical presence in the soul of the priest, it is clear that we must honor Christ's presence in every priest. It is easier to do so when a priest is willingly connected to that divine presence. It is more difficult, but more compelling I believe, to love the priests who are struggling.

Perhaps a priest is working against the kingdom. This is a dishonor to the covenant entered into by both God and the man at ordination. This is serious for the priest personally, of course, but also there is the gap in service and subsequent lag in the coming of God's Kingdom that results. The priest's non-service affects many. We must target these priests for rescue through love, intercessory prayer, and honest appeal.

Each reader must accept that I am not talking about assaulting a priest for his choice of spirituality. There are those who so love the path they have been called to in the Church that they believe that unless others are following that same path, others are getting it wrong. A priest does not have to be "into" this or that apostolate to be holy. A priest has to be "into" the presence of Christ in his priesthood.

What I am saying is that while it is good to introduce the priests in our lives to the spiritual movements that are helping us, we should not make judgments about these priests based on their acceptance or non-acceptance of a particular spiritual movement.

There is something so beautiful about the priests that I have seen in heaven. One particular priest I saw represented was not actually there yet. He was coming soon, but I saw his imprint in heaven, the shape of him in that his presence was evident through all of the fruits of his labor. There were many in heaven waiting for his arrival, people whose lives he has impacted through his vocation.

While the priest serves on earth, Jesus prepares his eternity. This is the same for all of us but priests have something different that endures for eternity. They have the mark of Christ on them in a more concrete way. Heaven is different because of this man's vocation and the vocation of every serving priest. Heaven is altered. There is more glory for God because this man allowed Christ to flow through him in administering the sacraments and providing assistance to others with regard to direction, affirmation, and confirmation of what is God's will and what is not God's will.

It strikes me that the priesthood is under a ferocious attack. The sins of a few have been used by the enemy in an attempt to strip the dignity from many. Nobody can strip dignity from another, though, least of all from a man who shares the divine priesthood with Jesus Christ. I am keenly aware of the dignity of the men who are ordained priests. I am also aware of their sinfulness in the same way as they are aware of the sinfulness of others in that we are all asked to serve in our humanity, but I understand that their humanity can provide them with the humility to make them beautiful in God's eyes. How God loves them and rejoices in them.

I would encourage each priest to rejoice in his humanity, just as God does. And just as each priest should rejoice in his humanity, and at the same time, each priest should rejoice in the divinity of Jesus Christ and in the divine nature of Christ present in his vocation.

Sinfulness, the propensity toward sin, is not a problem for Jesus. He can work through us in spite of our human nature which pulls us to selfishness. I see priests working and I see God's presence. They are connected, God and the man. They are united. The Father's eyes do not leave the priest because the Father's Son is within the soul of the priest and His goals, the Father's, rest in the heart of the Son. The Father's love for each child on earth is contained in the Son which is then transmitted into the heart of each priest. Truly, only in heaven will the priest see the scope of what God places in his soul at ordination.

Nobody can strip the dignity from a man such as this.

A priest should never worry about his humanity, as I said. He should fight always to resist temptation of course, but he should understand that Christ will always be good and His goodness resides in the priest. When the priest falls, Christ remains standing. Christ will not stop being good simply because we stop being good. It is this that should comfort us when we are tempted toward discouragement because of our ongoing imperfection.

How does Jesus feel about His priests? How can we make a comparison in human terms that will do justice to the feelings of the Savior for these men?

Imagine first how the Father felt toward Jesus. Jesus was His beloved one, of one and the same divinity, perfectly committed to the will and goals of the Father despite terrific hardship. At total personal cost, Jesus pursued the Father's goals.

The Father's goals often did not make sense to those who worked with Jesus. The world viewed Jesus as foolish at times. The world persecuted Christ. Christ persevered despite everything. Nothing the world threw at Christ diverted Him from the path the Father had chosen for Him.

Imagine how the Father viewed His Son.

The Father views each priest in the same way. They are part of Him as Jesus is part of Him. Each priest will rest with the Father in His heart. Not near His heart, but in His heart because truly when a priest pursues ordination, he is pursuing oneness with God.

Jesus Christ shares a brotherhood with each priest. He stands with the priest, in union with God and through the Holy Spirit. When the priest speaks for God, God sends the grace to accompany the words. The fact that the recipient of the priest's speech and counsel may not be open to the Holy Spirit present in his words in a given moment or in an immediate moment in no way diminishes the divine at work.

In other words, the priest cannot take a lack of receptivity on the part of those to whom he speaks as evidence that he, the priest, is either ineffective or lacking the presence of Christ in his vocation.

This is important, particularly during this time when so many do not serve. I see that some priests are discouraged and do not proceed with an awareness of their value to each of us, a value which has eternal consequences. The fact that people do not recognize the truth is no reason to stop speaking the truth because someday, with God's grace and when they are ready, these people will think back to the words of the priest and they will recognize these words as truth.

One who sows seeds must be content to leave the seeds to germinate at the correct time. It is for the farmer to reap the harvest and Jesus Christ Himself will collect the harvest at the appropriate time for each soul.

Priests must always look to Christ and His experience on earth. Did Christ always feel effective in His teaching and preaching?

Well, after Christ spoke the truth to Pilate, the people crucified Him. Does this mean Christ was ineffective and His service and suffering pointless and fruitless? Clearly not.

In the same way, often a priest will be denied immediate gratification in terms of witnessing the fruits of his labor, just as Christ, in His humanity, did not live to see what His three years of preaching and ultimate death on the cross would achieve. The priest, at ordination, agrees to share in this service and sacrifice and accepts that unlike an earthly bridge builder, he will not usually see the end result of his work until he reaches eternity.

This is all the more reason why the eternity of each priest will delight us. We will then certainly see the bridges built by each priest. We will see the elaborate benefits and interconnecting graces that pulled many of us back into the safety net of the family of God or that protected many of us from falling out of the safety net of the family of God. Indeed, only then will we see the intricate safety nets woven for us by each priest in his daily "yes" to Jesus Christ. How their constant labors represent God's love for each of us and how their daily service speaks to us of God's love present in each one of them. Oh, dear. It is so very clear that we do not love them enough.

In heaven, we will be filled with awe at the power of goodness that the Lord allowed to burst into the world in each daily Mass.

In heaven we will see the spectacular healings that took place through the Sacrament of Confession and the great calm that washed over anguished souls at the encounters with Christ they experienced through the Anointing of the Sick.

How grateful we will be in heaven when we witness what happened in our moment of Baptism and at our Confirmations.

At the other end of each of these experiences is a man, serving in his humanity.

Truly, each priestly act will be part of that priest's eternity and we will rejoice with each priest and for each priest at the reward he enjoys for his service to the kingdom.

I have often said that many priests underestimate the influence and impact they have on those they serve. For Catholics, the priestly presence is knitted into the most pivotal experiences of our lives.

Consider our First Holy Communion, Confirmation, Marriage, the Baptism of our children, the death of our loved ones, our own deaths. These life-changing moments are presided over by Christ through a priest. People remember with such gratitude the presence of the priest at the bedside of a dying family member and at their funerals. People, often in brokenness, look to the priest to make sense out of some of the tragic circumstances experienced during our time on earth.

Far from feeling unable or unequal to the task, the priest should accept that he, in his humanity, could disappoint, but Christ, in His divinity, will never disappoint. In other words, to repeat an important thought, the priest can rejoice and be at peace in the limitations of his humanity while constantly proclaiming the power of Christ's divinity.

Our Lady said that we are giving her the greatest pleasure by illuminating the divine presence of her Son in each priestly vocation. Our Lady is devoted to each of her children but she pays special attention to the needs of God's beloved priests.

I see that each priest is different as each man is different. Their unique character is designed by God for the service He requires from them. God takes all of their attributes and, with the most gentle tap of a divine touch, sanctifies them.

If a priest desires holiness, he must turn inward, to Jesus Christ in his soul.

The flame of divine love burns steadily in each priest. The more a priest turns his eyes inward, to Christ, the greater the amount of God's love that can flow through him.

We are each this way, of course. The more we climb our mountain of holiness, the more effectively Christ can use us.

There is something different about the priesthood, though. The mark of Jesus Christ, or shall we call it the stamp of the First Priest, predisposes the man to becoming transformed into another Christ. In order to cooperate with this transformation, a priest has to desire to be like Christ. I do not believe that every man ordained necessarily possesses a passionate desire for this transformation. I believe that this desire can come and grow and become compelling as the priest comes to know Christ through his ministry or through his suffering and sacrifice, or indeed through whatever circumstances God allows for him. God Himself will fuel this desire for transformation, particularly when He is asked.

Transformation, by its nature, demands change. St. Paul speaks to this.

"It is no longer I who live, but Christ who lives in me" (Gal 2:20).

This is the goal. This transformation from one man, the

priest, to another, Christ, requires that one of the two participants must change. Clearly, Jesus Christ who is God cannot change. It is not even possible. So it is the man who must change. The priest has to constantly reduce his will, making it smaller and smaller until it disappears altogether. You might say that this transformation is actually a process of reduction. The priest in his daily "yes" to Jesus cooperates with the shrinking of his human will. John the Baptist knew this.

"He must increase but I must decrease" (John 3:30).

Yes, the human will in each priest has to go where it does not match the divine will. It, self-will, must be jettisoned, sacrificed to the process of unity with Christ in service to the Father for the good of the Body of Christ and for God's greater glory. Only the will of the Father should remain for the man to be authentically Jesus Christ.

If this process, this transformation, were to rely on the priest, it would not even be worth embarking upon, so obviously impossible would it both appear and actually be. But this process relies on Jesus Christ.

The priest must allow himself to be grafted to the vine that is Christ.

"I am the true vine, and My Father is the vinedresser…Abide in Me, and I in you. As the branch cannot bear fruit by itself, unless it abides in the vine, neither can you, unless you abide in Me. I am the vine, you are the branches. He who abides in Me, and I in him, he it is that bears much fruit, for apart from Me you can do nothing" (John 15:1, 4-5).

Consider please that the act of allowing oneself to be grafted to the will of another is heroic, all by itself. It is an acknowledgement by a man that alone he is of less value than he will be if he is attached to the divine. This acknowledgement, when made with honesty, is a lovely and sublime act of humility that enables Christ to begin the transformation. You might say, actually, that this acknowledgement is the beginning of the transformation.

Pride is the enemy of this acknowledgement, of course, but this is not a work on pride, but on the power of Jesus Christ to transform and as the self-will diminishes, so does the pride.

We ask God constantly for the discernment to identify His will, then reduce our will and replace it with the divine will. That is the daily goal, the ongoing cooperation with the process of transformation.

I understand that God's priests are called to this process in a profound way. I do not have words to distinguish the call to holiness that is the priest's from that of a lay person or even a female religious, but I know that there is something here that, like Our Lady's role, is distinct. I am in no way minimizing the heroic call to holiness of others. I am simply concentrating in this moment on the call to the priesthood.

A priest offers his whole life for service to us, God's children. How many of us look to Jesus and say, "Take my life, Lord. Use it. I am willing to sacrifice myself so that my brothers and sisters might know You and be saved?"

This is what a priest gives to God for us, his whole life.

Brothers and sisters, this is a complete sacrifice. Jesus, always mindful of nourishing the Body of Christ, accepts each of these offerings with indescribable reverence and hope. He understands that the man who offers himself to the priesthood is giving everything in the name of the Invisible Reality. This is such a big offering. Can we take it in at all? Possibly not. Possibly this will require the divine vision that is available to us only after we die in our bodies.

I am at peace with the inability to understand the scope of this offering but our limited understanding should not prevent us from marvelling at and seeking to protect each vocation to the priesthood.

To make another point about the Lord's experience of an offering made by a man of his life in the priesthood, I view it from a different angle. I believe that when a man is ordained, when he enters this covenant, Jesus understands completely where the man experiences weakness. Jesus understands completely where the man is likely to trip and fall. Jesus sees both the strengths and the weaknesses in the man and Jesus provides the priest with His own kind of safety net. Jesus will literally wrap the priest in protection so that he does not do damage. The priest accepts this protection by committing to prayer and a disciplined prayer life. If the priest denies Jesus access, in other words, does not pray, Jesus is limited in the amount of protection He can give the priest and the priest is then more likely to do damage to the goals of God.

Now we must be clear that when Jesus acts through the priest in a sacramental way, heaven's goals are protected. The priest need not be particularly holy or indeed even in the state of grace for the validity of the sacrament performed by and through the priest. What I am saying is that if a priest is connected to Christ through prayer and silence, through a willingness to reduce his human will and replace it with the Lord's will, that priest will be better able to express and distribute God's mercy and love in his service. It can be no other way and the love of the First Priest will be communicated to others through each successive priest.

To be even more clear, I will say it this way. Others have told me that they can only confess to one priest because only this one priest understands them. I accept that certain personalities work well together and I accept that the methods of one priest may appeal to a given person more than the methods of another. At the same time, if I needed to have my Confession heard, I would go to any priest in complete confidence, regardless of the apparent condition of the priest.

The Lord is present in each priest. Each of us can trust in His presence.

To make a final point on this, most of us, priests included, have been exposed to priests who speak and act against the teaching of the Church. Clearly, if a priest is exhorting others to be disobedient to the Church or Church teaching, or if a priest himself is behaving sinfully or in a way that is disobedient to Church teaching, we can be sure that we are dealing with the self-will of the priest and not the divine will. Even in these cases though, the sacraments performed by the priest are valid and the sacramental graces present.

I see that Jesus loves His priests most tenderly. His plan for renewal rests in the hearts of His priests.

If Jesus Christ wills a renewal for the world, and He does, a renewal will occur. Each of us must determine our individual role in the renewal with a great determination to serve to the fullest possible extent, thereby maximizing the Lord's reach through our individual commitment.

When we are beginning to serve to a fuller extent, giving the Lord a more total "yes", we will feel stretched. Jesus calls us to surpass our intended line of service and step out into the unknown with Him. There is often a temptation to remain safely within what is comfortable for us but this is not good and we should be alert to this natural human proclivity. We will be comfortable in heaven for eternity, after all. We must accept some discomfort during our time on earth.

I would urge priests to rejoice in God's presence. Rejoice in God's plan. Each priest must strive to rejoice in God's choosing of him for such glorious service to the kingdom, even though that service is often cloaked in the most humble of tasks. The call to rejoicing is an imperative for priests because only through rejoicing can they proclaim Christ with any accuracy.

Some might question whether or not rejoicing is possible in a time when the Church is suffering so badly in many areas. But Christ has not abandoned His Church. Christ is truly present in each one of us who loves Him. Heaven has not changed. There is great rejoicing in heaven and there is great rejoicing on earth by anyone who is connected to the Lord in his soul.

God's Kingdom comes and rejoicing is in order.

Each priest must look honestly into his soul. In his soul, he will find the eyes of Christ. When one meets the divine gaze, one is strengthened and confirmed in service. A priest makes a commitment to an Invisible Reality, that is, Jesus Christ truly present in his ministry. Well, it is abundantly clear then that Jesus Christ must be *allowed* to be truly present in the ministry of each priest.

Fathers, increase your prayer time. Nourish your prayer life. Scrutinize your personal relationship with the Lord because it is only through this relationship that rejoicing can occur.

Rejoice. Proclaim.

The priest must connect himself to Jesus Christ and rejoice in the Lord's presence. We are called to bring Good News, not bad news. The world brings bad news to God's children in a steady flow. We, who are called to be different, must accept personally that God has not left us and that God has a need for fidelity in this time as He does in every other time.

We will move from an Age of Disobedience to an Age of Obedience and we will do this through one person at a time.

God's beloved priests will set an example of obedience, both in thought and action.

When one is being attacked unjustly, there is a temptation to respond in a defensive way, with anger. This is human nature. We, as followers of Christ, must reject our human nature and respond with God's divine nature. We must try to rest in God's truth, refusing to become discouraged by the fact that falseness appears to abound. The first apostles were consistently persecuted.

"We are in difficulties on all sides, but never cornered; we see no answer to our problems, but never despair; we have been persecuted, but never deserted; knocked down, but never killed; always, wherever we may be, we carry with us in our body the death of Jesus, so that the life of Jesus, too, may always be seen in our body" (Corinthians 4:8-10).

Yes, it is clear that the early apostles struggled. It is also clear, though, that they expected no less. They understood that if they were called to follow Jesus they would be treated like Jesus, whose experience included mockery and anguish.

"So they went on their way from the presence of the Council, rejoicing that they had been considered worthy to suffer shame for His name. And every day in the temple and from house to house, they kept right on teaching and preaching Jesus as the Christ" (Acts 5: 41-42).

The priesthood is being attacked in this time, both directly and indirectly. There is no shortage of ignorance from those who seek to avoid God's will in their own lives. In many areas, this has created for priests an atmosphere where it is difficult to rejoice and proclaim.

Beloved Fathers of God's children, the enemy offers shame and bitterness from this purification, it is true. But at the same time, God offers humility and gentleness. We are not bound to accept the ugly fruits of the enemy's efforts. We can reject despair and feelings of futility.

We are bound instead to accept the bountiful fruits of the renewal. If we do so, we will never be trapped in helplessness by the shocking pain of the sins committed by the few.

We must rejoice in God's presence and allow the Lord to bring healing and renewal to each of us personally. Jesus will do this for each of us. Truly, I am certain that each priest will experience a burst of joy if He asks for it.

This renewal, this commitment to personal transformation will produce humility and great heavenly calm. Christ will possess each priestly vocation to a degree that will delight each priest, creating an invulnerable protection against the temptations of the times.

Truly, God's desire to renew the priesthood is passionate.

When one feels passionate about something, one very often gives to a degree that appears to exceed common thinking and expectation.

I believe God is passionately committed to a renewal of holiness in His priests. Today's priests must be equally passionate about abandoning themselves to the cause of the Church. They must be as committed as the first apostles.

The combination of God's passionate desire to renew the priesthood with the priest's passionate commitment to proclaiming Christ will draw the renewal down into the world like nothing else.

Rejoice in God's presence. Proclaim His presence to the world.

Mary, our mother, is available to us in each moment. She serves faithfully with Jesus, calling out most particularly to priests. She watches, ever vigilant, for every opportunity to protect and defend each priest. She, in her feminine way, makes available to each priest an example of gentle nurturing, the same nurturing that she uses with each of her children.

It seems to me that Our Lady was granted union with God here on earth and as such there was no wrenching process necessary for her to move from humanity to eternity. This was a sublime graciousness on the part of God. He bestowed all that heaven had to offer on her. For Our Lady, the heavenly union was achieved, through her willingness and cooperation and through God's great graciousness, on earth. We all experience union with Christ in heaven in the same way that Our Lady experiences union with Christ in heaven but she is different.

I am not saying Our Lady is divine. For clarity let me say that I see this as a vision. Our Lady was conceived mystically in the heart of the Father. From that heart, she proceeded into the world. Her heart never separated from God's heart. When it was time, He glanced at her. She knew Him immediately in this mystical way and accepted His Son, God, into her body as a human mother but also into her soul as one who experiences union in heaven. So at the moment of the Lord's physical conception, the Incarnation, Our Lady became like one who enters heaven. She achieved union, through necessity and desire on God's part, and willingness and longing on her part, like the saint who is taken up into permanent residence in heaven. Only she remained on earth. As a concession and reward and as a way of making her stand out as God's human temple, God brought her into heaven at the end of her life just the way she was, in this perpetual spiritual union.

I don't know how to clarify this except to say that Our Lady stands out as God's chosen Queen of heaven and earth. This is huge. Who is above her? Only the Trinity. Her role will never be repeated. As such, she would merit very close study.

Every time I talk about Our Lady, I come to the priesthood. It is like an intellectual cul de sac for me. I think I am trying to distinguish between Our Lady's union with God and God's presence in the priesthood.

Our Lady had perfect purity. Priests serving in their humanity do not. God's giving the priest a share of His divinity at ordination is something different from what Our Lady experienced and yet I believe it is comparable in many ways. I see a similarity between what happened to Mary at the Incarnation and what happens to a priest at Ordination

I believe it was very important for God to show us how to live. It was for this reason He sent Christ. He sent Christ as the ideal for humanity in male form. I believe Our Lady is the ideal for humanity in female form. While she was not perfect as God is perfect, she perfectly represents God's presence in a woman. Just as we all, both men and women, should strive to be like Jesus in character and behavior, we should also strive to be like Mary in character and behavior.

I believe Mary must be God's most favored servant. She is the Saint Among Saints, the epitome of the servant of God. Many saints have bestowed upon them by God high levels of unity or even union while they remain on earth.

I believe with great certainty that none compare to Mary.

A priest who studies the gentleness and obedience of Mary will make great gains in the authentic representation of her Son.

Almighty God,
Father of our Lord Jesus Christ,
to You I pledge my allegiance
and the service of my entire life.
Grant me the help of Your Spirit
to live like Mary, my Mother,
in perfect obedience to Your holy will.
Amen.

Prayer written by a priest for priests.

Guidelines for Lay Apostles
of Jesus Christ the Returning King

Guidelines for Lay Apostles

As lay apostles of Jesus Christ the Returning King, we agree to perform our basic obligations as practicing Catholics. Additionally, we will adopt the following spiritual practices, as best we can:

1. **Allegiance Prayer** and **Morning Offering**, plus a brief prayer for the Holy Father
2. **Eucharistic Adoration**, one hour per week
3. **Prayer Group Participation**, monthly, at which we pray the Luminous Mysteries of the Holy Rosary and read the Monthly Message
4. **Monthly Confession**
5. Further, we will follow the example of Jesus Christ as set out in the Holy Scripture, treating all others with His patience and kindness.

Allegiance Prayer

Dear God in Heaven, I pledge my allegiance to You. I give You my life, my work and my heart. In turn, give me the grace of obeying Your every direction to the fullest possible extent. Amen.

Morning Offering

O Jesus, through the Immaculate Heart of Mary, I offer You the prayers, works, joys and sufferings of this day, for all the intentions of Your Sacred Heart, in union with the Holy Sacrifice of the Mass throughout the world, in reparation for my sins, and for the intentions of the Holy Father. Amen.

Prayer for the Holy Father

Blessed Mother of Jesus, protect Our Holy Father Benedict XVI, and bless all of his intentions.

Five Luminous Mysteries

1. The Baptism of Jesus
2. The Wedding at Cana
3. The Proclamation of God's Kingdom
4. The Transfiguration
5. The Institution of the Eucharist

Promise from Jesus to His Lay Apostles

May 12, 2005

Your message to souls remains constant. Welcome each soul to the rescue mission. You may assure each lay apostle that just as they concern themselves with My interests, I will concern Myself with theirs. They will be placed in My Sacred Heart and I will defend and protect them. I will also pursue complete conversion of each of their loved ones. So you see, the souls who serve in this rescue mission as My beloved lay apostles will know peace. The world cannot make this promise as only heaven can bestow peace on a soul. This is truly heaven's mission and I call every one of heaven's children to assist Me. You will be well rewarded, My dear ones.

The Volumes

*Direction for Our Times
as given to Anne, a lay apostle*

These books are available at
www.directionforourtimes.com
or at your local bookstore.

The *Heaven Speaks* Booklets

Direction for Our Times
as given to Anne, a lay apostle

These booklet are from the series *Direction for Our Times as given to Anne, a lay apostle*. They are available individually from Direction for Our Times and are listed below:

Heaven Speaks About Abortion

Heaven Speaks About Addictions

Heaven Speaks to Victims of Clerical Abuse

Heaven Speaks to Consecrated Souls

Heaven Speaks About Depression

Heaven Speaks About Divorce

Heaven Speaks to Prisoners

Heaven Speaks to Soldiers

Heaven Speaks About Stress

Heaven Speaks to Young People

New in 2007:

Heaven Speaks to Those Away from the Church

Heaven Speaks to Those Considering Suicide

Heaven Speaks to Those Who Are Dying

Heaven Speaks to Those Who Do Not Know Jesus

Heaven Speaks to Those Who Experience Tragedy

Heaven Speaks to Those Who Fear Purgatory

Heaven Speaks to Those Who Have Rejected God

Heaven Speaks to Those Who Struggle to Forgive

Heaven Speaks to Those Who Suffer from Financial Need

Heaven Speaks to Parents Who Worry About Their Children's Salvation

More books by Anne, a lay apostle

Climbing the Mountain
The Mist of Mercy

Interviews with Anne, a lay apostle

VHS tapes and DVDs featuring Anne, a lay apostle, have been produced by Focus Worldwide Network and can be purchased by visiting our website at www.directionforourtimes.com.